Sim

by Iain Gray

LangSyne

PUBLISHING

WRITING *to* REMEMBER

79 Main Street, Newtongrange,
Midlothian EH22 4NA
Tel: 0131 344 0414   Fax: 0845 075 6085
E-mail: info@lang-syne.co.uk
www.langsyneshop.co.uk

Design by Dorothy Meikle
Printed by Ricoh Print Scotland
© Lang Syne Publishers Ltd 2012

ISBN 978-1-85217-201-5

Simpson

Echoes of a far distant past
can still be found in most names

Chapter one:

Origins of Scottish surnames

by George Forbes

It all begun with the Normans.

For it was they who introduced surnames into common usage more than a thousand years ago, initially based on the title of their estates, local villages and chateaux in France to distinguish and identify these landholdings, usually acquired at the point of a bloodstained sword.

Such grand descriptions also helped enhance the prestige of these arrogant warlords and generally glorify their lofty positions high above the humble serfs slaving away below in the pecking order who only had single names, often with Biblical connotations as in Pierre and Jacques.

The only descriptive distinctions among this peasantry concerned their occupations, like Pierre the swineherd or Jacques the ferryman.

The Normans themselves were originally Vikings (or Northmen) who raided, colonised and eventually settled down around the French coastline.

They had sailed up the Seine in their longboats in 900AD under their ferocious leader Rollo and ruled the roost in north east France before sailing over to conquer England, bringing their relatively new tradition of having surnames with them.

It took another hundred years for the Normans to percolate northwards and surnames did not begin to appear in Scotland until the thirteenth century.

These adventurous knights brought an aura of chivalry with them and it was said no damsel of any distinction would marry a man unless he had at least two names.

The family names included that of Scotland's great hero Robert De Brus and his compatriots were warriors from families like the De Morevils, De Umphravils, De Berkelais, De Quincis, De Viponts and De Vaux.

As the knights settled the boundaries of

their vast estates, they took territorial names, as in Hamilton, Moray, Crawford, Cunningham, Dunbar, Ross, Wemyss, Dundas, Galloway, Renfrew, Greenhill, Hazelwood, Sandylands and Church-hill.

Other names, though not with any obvious geographical or topographical features, nevertheless derived from ancient parishes like Douglas, Forbes, Dalyell and Guthrie.

Other surnames were coined in connection with occupations, castles or legendary deeds. Stuart originated in the word steward, a prestigious post which was an integral part of any large medieval household. The same applied to Cooks, Chamberlains, Constables and Porters.

Borders towns and forts – needed in areas like the Debateable Lands which were constantly fought over by feuding local families – had their own distinctive names; and it was often from them that the resident groups took their communal titles, as in the Grahams of Annandale, the Elliots and Armstrongs of the East Marches, the Scotts and Kerrs of Teviotdale and Eskdale.

Even physical attributes crept into surnames, as in Small, Little and More (the latter being 'beg' in Gaelic), Long or Lang, Stark, Stout, Strong or Strang and even Jolly.

Mieklejohns would have had the strength of several men, while Littlejohn was named after the legendary sidekick of Robin Hood.

Colours got into the act with Black, White, Grey, Brown and Green (Red developed into Reid, Ruddy or Ruddiman). Blue was rare and nobody ever wanted to be associated with yellow.

Pompous worthies took the name Wiseman, Goodman and Goodall.

Words intimating the sons of leading figures were soon affiliated into the language as in Johnson, Adamson, Richardson and Thomson, while the Norman equivalent of Fitz (from the French-Latin 'filius' meaning 'son') cropped up in Fitzmaurice and Fitzgerald.

The prefix 'Mac' was 'son of' in Gaelic and clans often originated with occupations – as in MacNab being sons of the Abbot, MacPherson and MacVicar being sons of the minister and MacIntosh being sons of the chief.

The church's influence could be found in the names Kirk, Clerk, Clarke, Bishop, Friar and Monk. Proctor came from a church official, Singer and Sangster from choristers, Gilchrist and Gillies from Christ's servant, Mitchell, Gilmory and Gilmour from servants of St Michael and Mary, Malcolm from a servant of Columba and Gillespie from a bishop's servant.

The rudimentary medical profession was represented by Barber (a trade which also once included dentistry and surgery) as well as Leech or Leitch.

Businessmen produced Merchants, Mercers, Monypennies, Chapmans, Sellers and Scales, while down at the old village watermill the names that cropped up included Miller, Walker and Fuller.

Other self explanatory trades included Coopers, Brands, Barkers, Tanners, Skinners, Brewsters and Brewers, Tailors, Saddlers, Wrights, Cartwrights, Smiths, Harpers, Joiners, Sawyers, Masons and Plumbers.

Even the scenery was utilised as in Craig, Moor, Hill, Glen, Wood and Forrest.

Rank, whether high or low, took its place with Laird, Barron, Knight, Tennant, Farmer, Husband, Granger, Grieve, Shepherd, Shearer and Fletcher.

The hunt and the chase supplied Hunter, Falconer, Fowler, Fox, Forrester, Archer and Spearman.

The renowned medieval historian Froissart, who eulogised about the romantic deeds of chivalry (and who condemned Scotland as being a poverty stricken wasteland), once sniffily dismissed the peasantry of his native France as the jacquerie (or the jacques-without-names) but it was these same humble folk who ended up overthrowing the arrogant aristocracy.

In the olden days, only the blueblooded knights of antiquity were entitled to full, proper names, both Christian and surnames, but with the passing of time and a more egalitarian, less feudal atmosphere, more respectful and worthy titles spread throughout the populace as a whole.

Echoes of a far distant past can still be found in most names and they can be borne with pride in commemoration of past generations who fought and toiled in some capacity or other to make our nation what it now is, for good or ill.

Chapter two:

The kindred of Simon

Stemming as it does from the forename Simon or Sim, and meaning 'son of Simon', or 'son of Sim', the surname Simpson in Scotland would appear to derive from two separate sources.

Introduced by the Normans following their conquest of England in 1066, Simon became a popular forename, or Christian, name and later developed into a hereditary surname in variations that in Scotland included Semsoun, Semssoune, Simsoun, Symsoun, Simpsone, Symon, and Syme.

To bear the name Simpson indicates you are 'of the kindred of Simon', but there were several such 'kindreds of Simon'. In Scotland, two of these in particular came to dominate the two distinct geographical locations of the Lowlands and the Highlands.

Those Simpsons who settled in the

Lowlands can trace their roots, through a rather tangled genealogical skein, back to Archil, a mighty Saxon lord who flourished in what is now the English county of Buckinghamshire, during the reign of Edward the Confessor (1004-1066).

Finding an accommodation with the Norman regime following the conquest of 1066, the family continued to thrive and one branch took the name of de Clint, after they acquired the manor of Clint, in Yorkshire.

They became so influential that they had their own crest of a lion and motto of 'Never despairing.'

By the late thirteenth and early fourteenth centuries a Simon de Clint, son of William de Clint, founded his own branch of the family and his descendants, accordingly, became known as 'the sons of Simon', or Simpson.

Branches of this 'kindred of Simon' later settled throughout the Borders, Lanarkshire, Ayrshire, and the Edinburgh area.

The Simpsons are also recognised as a

branch, or sept, of Clan Fraser, and some sources assert that this arose when some of the original 'de Clint' Simpsons later acquired lands in the north of Scotland and affiliated themselves with the clan.

This claim does not bear close scrutiny, however, but the possible truth behind the Simpson link with the Frasers is rather more interesting.

The Frasers trace their roots back to those Norman families who settled in England and later in Scotland following the Conquest of 1066.

By tradition the favoured baptismal name for sons of the Fraser family was 'Simon', to the extent that even today the Chief of the Frasers of Lovat is known in Gaelic as Mac Shimidh ('Son of Simon').

It was through this identification with the Fraser 'sons of Simon' that the Fraser kindred known as Simpson are thought to have arisen, while recognised septs of Clan Fraser include Simpson, Sims, Simson, Syme, Symon, Sim, and Simon.

As kindred of Clan Fraser, these 'sons of Simon' played a significant role in Scotland's turbulent history down through the centuries.

Simpsons who can trace a descent to Clan Fraser are heirs to a proud tradition. With the confident motto of 'All my hope is in God', and a crest of a flourish of strawberries, the Frasers have their roots in the French provinces of both Anjou and Normandy.

The colourful and decidedly botanical derivation of their name comes from 'fraise', the French word for strawberry, while strawberry plants are known as 'frasiers' – hence the name and clan crest.

It was in the late twelfth century when this family of Norman warriors who would become a distinguished Highland clan first came to Scotland, acquiring lands originally in Tweeddale, in the Borders, and then the north of the country particularly the Aberdeen, Angus, and Inverness areas.

The clan had several branches, one of which, the Frasers of Lovat, with a crest of a

Robert the Bruce, King of Scots — The Victor of Bannockburn

buck's head and motto of 'I am ready!' are recognised as a clan in their own proud right.

At the present day there are a number of Fraser tartans, including the Fraser of Lovat. While the Lovat Frasers may wear any of these tartans, only Lovat Frasers are entitled to wear the Lovat tartan.

The Frasers and their kinsfolk such as the Simpsons were at the forefront of Scotland's Wars of Independence with England, but it was a Fraser who unwittingly provided a spark that helped to light the flame of the long and bloody conflict.

This was William Fraser, Bishop of St. Andrews, who in 1290 made what would prove to be the fatal error of inviting Edward I of England to arbitrate over the vexed succession to the Scottish throne.

This followed the death of the heiress, the eight-year-old Margaret, the Maid of Norway, while she was en route to Scotland from the land of her birth.

Edward, who subsequently gained

infamy as 'the Hammer of the Scots', took the
invitation to mean he had superiority over the
northern kingdom and, accordingly, set about
imposing his authority with an iron fist.

Scotland rebelled, and during the conflict that ensued Sir Simon Fraser of
Tweeddale, known as 'the Patriot', joined the
forces of that great master of guerrilla warfare,
William Wallace.

Wallace had raised the banner of revolt
against English occupation of Scotland in May
of 1297, after he killed Sir William Heselrig,
Sheriff of Lanark, in revenge for the murder of
his young wife, Marion.

Wallace and his hardy band of freedom
fighters inflicted a series of defeats on the
heavily fortified English garrisons scattered
across Scotland, their success culminating in
the liberation of practically all of the country
following the battle of Stirling Bridge on
September 11, 1297.

Defeat followed at the battle of Falkirk
on July 22 of the following year and Wallace,

who had been entrusted as Guardian of Scotland, was betrayed and captured seven years later.

He was taken to London and brutally executed on the orders of Edward I.

Sir Simon Fraser rallied to the cause of Robert the Bruce, but paid dearly for his support for the cause of Scotland's freedom when he was captured and executed in 1306.

Sir Alexander Fraser, a relative of Sir Simon, fought at the side of Bruce at the battle of Bannockburn in 1314, when the Scots inflicted a resounding defeat on the cream of English chivalry under Edward II.

Sir Alexander Fraser was later rewarded by a grateful Bruce with the post of Lord Chamberlain.

Chapter three:

Raiders and rebels

**A William Symsoun of Edinburgh is record-
ed in 1405 as a wealthy burgess who, in all
probability, was engaged in the lucrative
wool trade with his de Clint/Simpson rela-
tives over the border in Yorkshire.**

While he was a respected and law-abid-
ing merchant, other Simspons had turned to less
legitimate enterprises in order to eke out a living.

In the late 1400s, Andro Semsoun and
Jock Semssoune are on record in Lanark for
theft and breach of the peace, while in the
Borders the Simpsons are recorded as being
among the 77 or so notorious reiving families
or 'riding clans.'

These reivers took their name from
their lawless custom of reiving, or raiding, not
only their neighbours' livestock, but also that
of their neighbours across the border.

The word 'bereaved', for example,

indicating to have suffered loss, derives from the original 'reived', meaning to have suffered loss of property.

The Treaty of York had been signed by Scotland's Alexander II in 1237, establishing the border with England as a line running from the Solway to the Tweed, but until as late as the seventeenth century the Borders became a byword for lawlessness.

There were three Marches, or areas of administration, on either side of the border – the West, Middle, and East Marches – all governed by a warden

In Scotland, the East March was dominated by the Homes and Swintons, with the Kerrs, Douglases, and Elliots holding sway in the Middle March, and the Armstrongs, Maxwells, and Johnstones in control of the West March.

The host of minor families, such as the Simpsons, allied themselves to particular stronger families, and shared in both their fortunes and misfortunes.

Complaints from either side of the border, and there were many, were dealt with on Truce Days, with the wardens of the respective marches acting as arbitrators.

Under a special law known as the Hot Trod, anyone who had their livestock stolen had the right to pursue the thieves and regain their property at the point of the sword.

In many cases, however, the wardens of the marches were far from arbitrary in their rulings, with self-interest governing their decisions, and as a result the Borders remained a scene of virtual anarchy, with no respect for royal authority.

This remained the case until James VI, following the Union of the Crowns in 1603, attempted to assert his authority.

It was a lengthy process. As late as 1608, one report submitted to the monarch lamented that 'wild incests, adulteries, convocation of the lieges, shooting and wearing of hackbutts, pistols and lances, daily bloodsheds, oppression, and disobedience in civil matters, neither are nor has been punished.'

As authority gradually began to assert

itself the power of the Border families such as the Simpsons was broken, many opting to seek a new life elsewhere.

Many of these Borders Simpsons settled elsewhere in the Lowlands and later in Ireland. From Ireland, many immigrated to North America, and that is why many American Simpsons of today can claim a Scottish descent, via Ireland.

There are records of a Robert Simpson in Salem, Massachusetts, in 1630, a Robert Simpson in Maryland in 1633, Henry Simpson in Maine in 1635, and Patrick Simpson in Virginia in 1639.

Many of Scotland's noble houses, clans, and simply ordinary families found themselves faced with a terrible conflict of conscience during the Jacobite Risings of 1715 and 1745.

While their hearts may have tugged at them to support the fortunes of the Royal House of Stuart, their heads told them that, faced with the military might and political power of the government that had strengthened since the

Act of Union of 1707, the wisest course was to opt for the status quo.

To throw in one's lot with the Jacobite cause was to risk death, exile, and the loss of title and lands through the processes known as attaintment and forfeiture.

Jacobite opposition to the succession to the throne in 1714 of George, the Elector of Hanover, was raised to such a pitch that on September 6, 1715, the Earl of Mar raised the banner of the exiled James VIII, and III, known as the Old Pretender, at Braemar.

A force of 10,000 men was raised, but the Jacobite cause was effectively lost after the battle of Sheriffmuir in November of 1715 when Mar retreated back to Perth, leaving the initiative with the Hanoverian forces led by John Campbell, 2nd Duke of Argyll.

Many of the clan chiefs who had rallied to the Old Pretender's standard later lost their titles and were forfeited, but not so the wily Simon Fraser, 11th Lord Lovat, known as the Fox because of his cunning.

He had opted to support the Hanoverian cause, even capturing the vital bastion of Stirling Castle for the government, but dissatisfaction over his subsequent treatment by the government led him thirty years later to throw in his lot with the Young Pretender, Prince Charles Edward Stuart, after he raised his Standard at Glenfinnan in August of 1745.

It was to prove a fatal move for Fraser, his clansmen, and his kinsfolk such as the Simpsons.

At the battle of Culloden, fought on Drummossie Moor, near Inverness, on April 16, 1746, Jacobite hopes were finally crushed under the disciplined artillery of the Hanoverian forces led by the Duke of Cumberland, later to earn the detested title of 'Butcher' Cumberland, because of the horrific cruelty inflicted in the aftermath of the battle.

The Frasers of Lovat are estimated to have lost up to 250 men at Culloden after charging with the right wing of the Jacobite army into the teeth of the deadly artillery.

At first sight, it is curious that the name Simpson is not listed under the Fraser of Lovat Regiment in the muster roll of the Jacobite army.

One interesting and rather curious explanation for this, however, may lie in the fact that the wily Simon Fraser of Lovat, in a bid to strengthen his position, had previously enlarged his already significant clan by 'adopting' what were known as 'Boll of Meal' Frasers.

These were men, including, perhaps, men who bore the name Simpson, who changed their name to Fraser in return for guaranteed food and shelter.

The surname Simpson, however, is found in the muster roll under a number of other Jacobite regiments that fought at Culloden.

Andrew Simpson, from Dundee, is listed as a drummer in the Forfarshire (Ogilvy's) Regiment, along with James Simpson, a 20-year-old shoemaker from Arbroath, John Simpson, a servant from Forfar, Patrick Simpson, a farmer from Forfar, and David Simpson, a weaver from Auldbar, near Brechin.

Simon Fraser, 11th Lord Lovat, was declared a traitor and rebel and beheaded on Tower Hill, London, in 1747, at the age of 90. He holds the dubious distinction of being the last peer to be executed in Britain.

His son, Simon, who fought with great bravery at Culloden, was deprived of both the estates and title he had inherited from his father, but these were returned to the family in 1857.

Beauly, in Invernesshire, remains the seat of the Frasers of Lovat.

Chapter four:

Easing the pain

Generations of Simpsons have gained both fame and a degree of infamy in a number of pursuits following the widespread discord of earlier centuries.

A huge debt is owed by the medical world to Sir James Young Simpson, born in Bathgate, in the east of Scotland, in 1811, and who pioneered the use of anaesthetics in surgical operations.

A landmark date in the history of medicine is January 19, 1847, when Simpson, who had studied at Edinburgh University, became the first to apply ether as an anaesthetic to reduce the pain of childbirth.

This was during the stern and strict Victorian age, and Simpson had to struggle against those who believed the use of anaesthetics was a crime against God and nature.

The vast majority of these opponents, needless to say, were men!

Sir James Young Simpson.

After experimenting with ether, Simpson discovered the anaesthetic properties of chloroform, the use of which became hugely popular after it was administered to Queen Victoria herself during the delivery of Prince Leopold in 1853.

Aged only 28, Simpson, who became the first person to be knighted for services to medicine, was appointed to the Chair of Midwifery at Edinburgh University.

In addition to radically improving the design of obstetrical forceps, he also pioneered techniques to reduce some of the fatal diseases often associated with childbirth.

Simpson had his own coat of arms, and his great achievements in medicine are aptly summed up in his personal motto of 'Victo Dolore' (Pain Conquered).

Thousands of people gathered for his funeral in Edinburgh, following his death in 1870, and he is buried in the city's Warriston Cemetery.

Born out of wedlock in about 1787 and raised by an aunt in Dingwall, in the north of Scotland, George Simpson overcame the disadvantages of his birth to become governor of the Hudson Bay Company in Canada and achieve the accolade of knighthood.

Aged in his early teens, he was sent from his native Scotland to work in an uncle's sugar brokerage in London, later obtaining a post with the North West Company.

Simpson was entrusted with one of the company's trading posts in Canada and, following the merger of the company with the Hudson Bay Company, he was appointed governor.

In addition to his duties as governor of the Hudson Bay Company, a post he held until

1856, Simpson explored vast tracts of Arctic Canada and from 1841 to 1842 made an arduous and celebrated expedition from Canada, across the frozen wastes of Siberia, to St. Petersburg. He died in 1860.

Orenthal James Simpson, born in San Francisco in 1947 and better known as O.J. Simpson, or 'The Juice', achieved celebrity not only as one of the most famous running backs in the history of American football, but as a sports commentator and as an actor.

He gained a rather more dubious celebrity, however, following a lengthy televised trial in which he was finally acquitted, in 1996, of the murder of his former wife, Nicole Brown, and her acquaintance Ronald Goldman – but a civil court found him liable for both deaths a year later.

On a happier note, a family of Simpsons have for several years enjoyed international fame as stars of a popular American television series actually named after them. Step forward the cartoon characters of Homer, Marge, Bart, Lisa, and Maggie, known and loved as *The Simpsons!*